andrea arden's

little book of dog tricks

andrea arden's

little book of dog tricks

by andrea arden illustrated by kristin doney

HOWELL
BOOK
HOUSE

Howell Book House

Published by Wiley Publishing, Inc., New York, NY

For general information on our other products and services or to obtain technical support please contact our Customer Care Department within the U.S. at 800-762-2974, outside the U.S. at 317-572-3993 or fax 317-572-4002.

Wiley also publishes its books in a variety of electronic formats. Some content that appears in print may not be available in electronic books.

Library of Congress Cataloging-in-Publication Data:

Arden, Andrea

Andrea Arden's little book of dog tricks / Andrea Arden; illustrated by Kristin Doney.

p. cm.

ISBN 0-7645-6634-2

1. Dogs–Training. 2. Clicker training (Animal training). 3. Games for dogs. I. Title.

SF431 .A754 2002

636.7'0835–dc21 2002010349

Manufactured in the United States of America

10 9 8 7 6 5 4 3 2 1

Book design by Sandy St. Jacques Cover design by Susan Olinsky

contents

list of games & tricks

chapter 1

benefits of teaching tricks

trick training is one of the best ways for you and your dog to have fun together, to build trust and confidence in each other and for you to show off to your friends and family just how smart your dog really is! But there are also some practical benefits.

Trick training provides mental exercise by asking your dog to become a creative thinker and to learn to understand you and what you want.

Tricks can also be a valuable source of physical exercise. Even simple tricks, such as "Wave" and "Roll Over," require your dog to expend energy and to use his muscles. Advanced tricks, such as "Sneaky Dog" and "Sit Pretty," offer even more in the way of a physical workout.

In addition, trick training improves attention, basic manners and obedience, and it may help to prevent and solve some behavior problems. After all, a dog who knows a repertoire of tricks has learned that people are very rewarding, especially when the dog pays attention to them and responds to their requests. A trained dog is also less likely to develop obedience or behavior problems like fear or aggression because he is more likely to be confident and well mannered.

In a nutshell, the goal of trick training is to have a blast with your dog so you can develop a canine companion who is a joy to live with.

my dog can do that?

Watching a professional trainer's dog run through a tricks routine might make anyone think that trick training is out of her league. The truth is, most tricks are very simple. In fact, as you read this book, you'll find that most tricks can be broken down into a few easy steps. Just be sure to talk to your veterinarian before beginning any new training or exercise regimen with your dog. That way, you can be sure to choose tricks that are appropriate for your dog's age, health and temperament.

playing the training game

When teaching tricks, the objective is for both you and your dog to have lots of fun. The best way to ensure good times—and to be a successful trick trainer—is to view training as a game. The "training game" is simple: Teach your dog that he gets all the things he wants in life from you (doggy resources), in exchange for good behavior (in this case, tricks). For example, food, toys and your attention can be earned in exchange for the tricks you teach your dog. If your dog understands this give-and-take, he will be eager to learn more ways to earn things from you. That is, your dog will be eager to learn more fun tricks!

motivation to play the training game

Any game is more fun when you have willing, motivated players. The training game is no exception. You are motivated to play because you know that trick training is fun and because it will result in a fantastic pet. You can motivate your dog to play by showing him that training is fun, by controlling all of the things he wants–the "doggy resources"–and by teaching him to earn these things in exchange for good behavior.

make playing the training game fun

There is no more effective way to make training fun than to adhere to the principles of modern, gentle dog trainers. The underlying principle of modern training is that you teach by using your brain rather than your brawn.

modern dog trainers:

- **Focus on teaching their dog good behavior rather than punishing for bad behavior.** For example, instead of punishing your dog for jumping up on people, why not simply teach him to sit to greet people?

- **Use gentle methods to teach.** There is no need to yank your dog around to get him to do what you want. In fact, training will glide along much more quickly and effectively if you don't use harsh physical force and punishments. For example, if you want to teach your dog to lie down on command, you needn't shove him to the ground. Instead, simply use a food lure to gently guide him into position (see "Lure It!", on page 27).

So toss out that old-fashioned choke collar, stop yelling "No!" and put on your thinking cap! You are about to become a terrific trainer who focuses on teaching her dog what she wants and then rewarding him for good behavior. Your dog will thank you for it—and you will be rewarded with a well-trained dog!

Using modern, gentle training methods is the best way to keep your dog interested in the training game. The following tips are also useful:

- **Keep training sessions short:** Generally speaking, sessions should be only about five minutes long. By keeping your training sessions brief, you have a good chance of ending the game while your dog still wants more attention, fun and training.

- **Reinforce often:** Be a generous "slot machine," and your dog is likely to become addicted to playing with you. But while you should generously offer rewards for good behavior, food treats should be very tiny in size (about half the size of a fingernail). This way, your dog is unlikely to get full (and a full dog isn't very motivated to play), get a tummy ache or even gain weight.
- **Be unpredictable:** Keep your dog guessing about what his reward will be. Surprising him with new rewards is a great way to keep your pooch interested in training. Talk to your veterinarian about food treats that are appropriate for your dog, and check out the doggy resources below for ideas about types of rewards that go beyond food.

control the doggy resources

Because you are focusing on making trick training a fun game, chances are your dog will enter the game with a good attitude. But he is even more likely to be motivated to play if you get control of all the things he wants and then ask him to make a deal: He gets what he wants in exchange for good behavior. Doggy resources can be broken down into four categories: food, toys, attention and life rewards.

food

Food includes your dog's normal meals and his special treats.

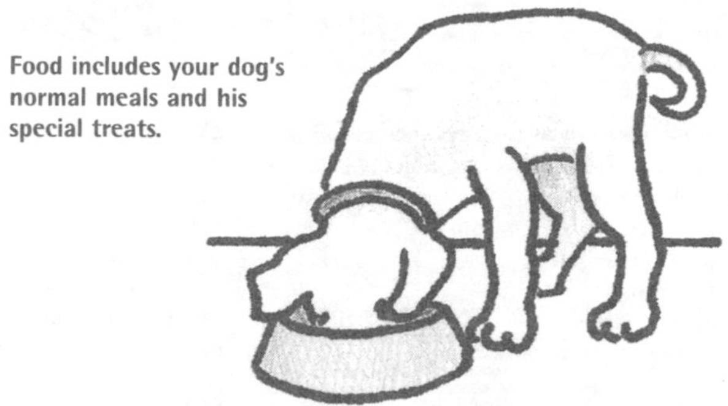

Break regular-sized treats into small pieces—you want to reward your dog, not fatten him up!

Keep an eye on your dog's chews and bones. Replace with new ones when they become worn.

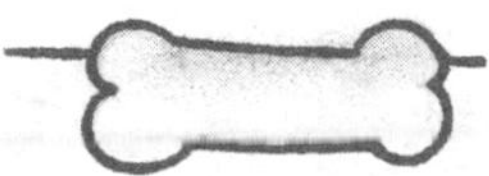

toys

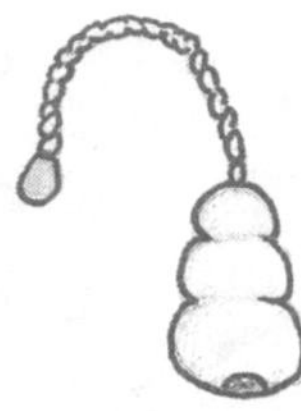

Kongs™ come in a number of sizes and styles—such as this one, on a rope. Hav-A-Balls are also a terrific, stuffable toy.

Toys include all of the objects your dog is allowed to play with.

Make sure you get dog toys that are size-appropriate. You don't want your big dog to choke on a too-small rubber ball—or your small dog to be intimidated by a very large toy.

attention

Attention is verbal and physical affection from people.

life rewards

Life rewards might include going out for walks, playing with other dogs, being allowed on the furniture and getting to ride in a car.

Two well-behaved dogs are better than one! Allow dogs to play together after you ask them to perform a trick—or two.

Observe your dog to discover his favorite life rewards. Your couch potato may not appreciate riding in the car or jogging through the park.

Obviously, your dog needs food, walks, chew toys and attention every single day. Controlling doggy resources doesn't mean depriving your dog of anything he got before you started training. It simply means changing your dog's perception of the doggy resources: You are convincing your dog that he is now getting those things in exchange for good behavior.

In the simplest terms, this means asking your dog to "Sit" before you put his food bowl on the ground. But take it a step further and ask him to lie down before you toss a squeaky toy for a game of fetch. Try asking for a "Sit" and a "Shake" before you open the front door to take him for a walk. And how about asking your dog to "Play Dead" before you scratch his ear?

Before you know it, your dog will use his brain to its fullest potential in an effort to figure out the best way to get what he wants.

Get control of the doggy resources and play the training game every day for a week, asking your dog to do a little something for each and every thing he wants. After just one week, both of you are sure to be skilled players in the training game.

where, when & how long to play the training game

It's best to begin dog training where there are as few distractions as possible, such as in your home. This way, your dog is much more likely to pay attention to you. This is especially true when you are teaching new behaviors that require your dog's full concentration.

When the behavior is reliable in your own home, start to practice it in slightly more distracting areas, such as the hallway of your apartment building or just outside your front door. Work toward reliability on walks, in the park and in other distracting environments. But when your dog is around other off-leash dogs, don't ask him to do too much. It is too much to ask any dog to "Sit Pretty" or "Roll Over" while another dog is playfully pouncing on him. In this case, your dog will likely opt out of the training game!

When you are playing the training game in an appropriate environment, it is best to restrict sessions to about five minutes each. This is especially true at the beginning of training. By keeping sessions brief, you can prevent frustration and boredom—for both you *and* your dog.

tools for the training game

You can train your dog with just a handful of tasty, healthy treats. But as with anything, the right equipment is sure to help things move along more smoothly.

a marker

One of the most important trick-training tools is something that tells your dog that what he is doing at a precise moment is *exactly* what you want him to do. For instance, if you want to teach your dog to sneeze on cue, you need a way to tell him it is the *exact* moment when he sneezes that will earn his reward. If he sneezes and you reach down to reward him for doing so without marking the behavior the moment it happens, chances are he won't make the connection between the sneeze and the reward—even if they are just a few seconds apart.

A great trick trainer knows it is important to be able to say—just as a behavior happens—"That's what I want! I'm giving you a treat because of *that* sneeze!" This is called "marking a behavior" because you have "marked" or pinpointed the exact behavior that earned the reward. But remember, the marker is not a command-giver or remote control for your dog. It is simply a way to give accurate feedback for good behavior.

A marker can be a word like "Yes!" or it can be the sound of a click from a clicker. Clickers were originally children's toys in the shape of frogs or crickets, but training clickers have evolved into small plastic rectangles that make a sharp clicking sound when you push down on one side of the metal interior.

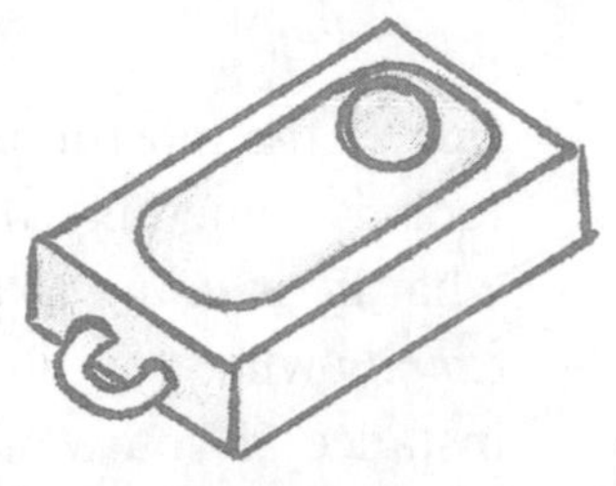

The sharp, clear sound of a training clicker is an accurate way of telling your dog that what he did at an exact moment is what earned him a reward. This is especially valuable for teaching more advanced tricks.

Some people prefer to use a verbal marker, the argument being that they always have their voices with them. However, most professional trainers use a clicker because clickers are more precise and clear than verbal markers. Also, the tone and pitch of your voice varies depending on your mood, whereas a clicker is always consistent. And, last but not least, a clicker is non-emotional and is unlikely to have preexisting negative associations, whereas your dog may perceive your voice to have some negative connotations even if you have just yelled "No!" a few times.

When your dog first hears the marker (a clicker, or your voice saying the word "Yes"), it probably won't mean much to him. But it's very easy to teach your dog that the marker means something good is coming. Simply make the sound (a click or "Yes!"), and then offer a tasty treat immediately after. *Immediate* is the key word here. Because food is a *primary* reinforcer, your dog doesn't need to be taught to appreciate it. But the marker is a *conditioned* reinforcer, meaning that you will need to *condition* (or teach) your dog to understand that the marker means something good (food) is coming.

When you first teach your dog what the marker means, you don't need to work on any specific behavior. Just make the sound and then offer a treat immediately afterward (or "mark and treat"). Do this for about 10 repetitions, moving around a bit as you do so. This way your dog will learn that it is the marker, not a specific spot, that means his reward is coming. After 10 to 20 repetitions, you can test your dog to see if he has made the association between the marker and the treat: Just make the sound and wait to see your dog's reaction. If he looks at you attentively, it's a good guess that he expects a treat and therefore understands what the marker means.

Note: Some dogs may be startled by the click. In this case, try muffling the sound by holding the clicker in your pocket. You can also have a friend or a family member click from another room and then you can reward your dog. It is worth the effort to teach your dog to make a positive association between the click and food, because a clicker is a valuable aid in trick training.

treat pouch

A good trainer is prepared to reward good behavior the moment it happens. Therefore, a good trainer has a sturdy treat pouch on hand for each training session. Most professional trainers use pouches with a plastic liner so they can carry around moist food without its leaking on their clothes. Some treat bags can be sealed with a zipper, drawstring or metal snap closure. Most pet stores carry one or two types of treat bags, but check out www.DogTraining101.com for the best sources of treat pouches.

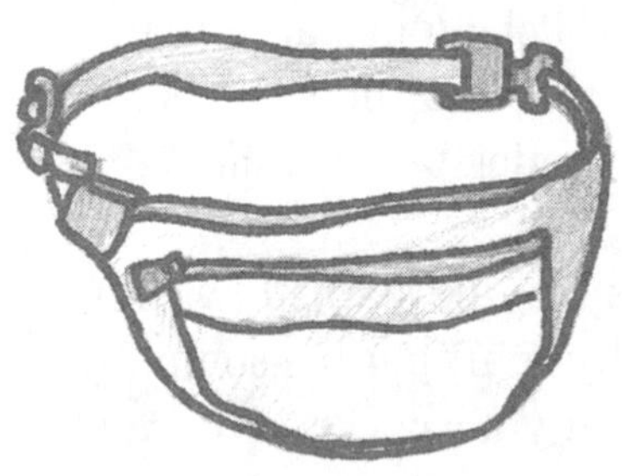

A treat pouch is a bag approximately four inches by five inches that can be attached to your waistband or through a belt loop.

a variety of rewards

They say variety is the spice of life, and that's certainly the case when it comes to dog-training treats. The best way to keep your dog motivated to play the training game is to use an assortment of rewards. It should come as no surprise that if you offer your dog the same treats day after day, you won't pique his interest for long. There are lots of terrific commercial treats on the market that can be used in addition to turkey cold cuts, hot dogs and some mild cheeses. However, please consult your veterinarian to make sure that your choices are appropriate and safe for your dog.

Regardless of the type of food you use, the pieces should be tiny little crumbs, about half the size of your fingernail. This way your dog works hard for a small amount, isn't likely to get full quickly and isn't likely to gain weight.

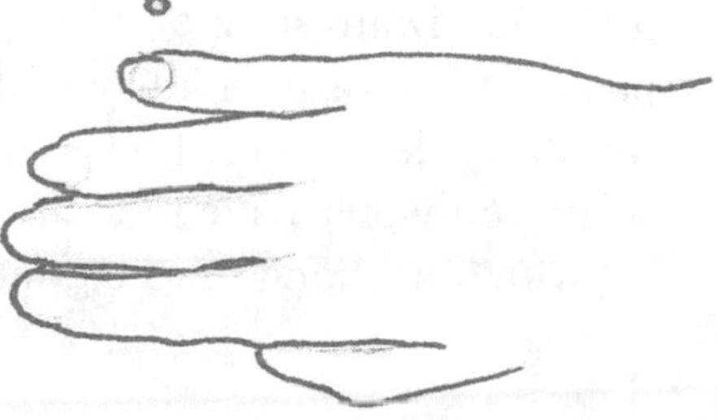

Treats should be no larger than half the size of your fingernail.

a target stick

A target can be any object you teach your dog to move toward and touch with his nose. Most trainers teach their dogs to target to their hand and to a target stick.

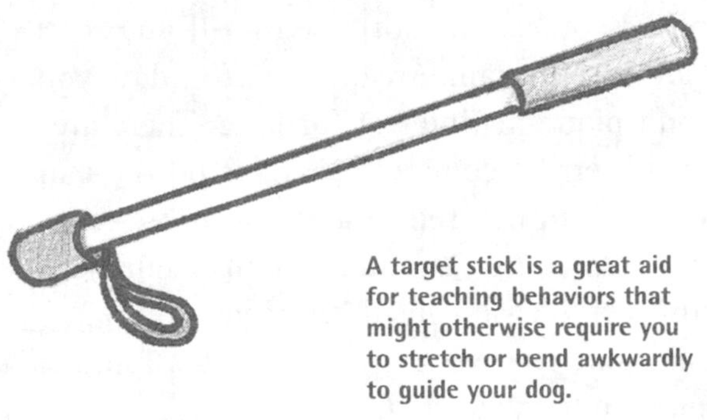

A target stick is a great aid for teaching behaviors that might otherwise require you to stretch or bend awkwardly to guide your dog.

A target stick is usually about two-and-a-half feet long and can be purchased from such pet suppliers as www.DogTraining101.com. Alternatively, you can use a wooden dowel from a hardware store or a long wooden spoon from your own kitchen. If you want to teach your dog to crawl, using a target stick means you won't have to clumsily guide your dog with your hand on the ground.

creative cues/commands

Cues and commands are two ways of saying the same thing: a request for your dog to perform a specific behavior. Part of the fun of trick training is coming up with creative names or cues for tricks. For example, teaching your dog to roll onto his side and lay still is cute if you say, "Lie on your side." But it is even cuter if you teach your dog to lie on his side when you say "Bang!"

adding cues/commands

It may surprise some people to find out that cues should not be introduced at the beginning of training. The traditional way of training is to say the cue as you are trying to get a behavior–for example, to say "Sit!" as you begin to show the dog what you want "Sit" to mean. But it is actually best to wait until you are sure you can get a behavior before assigning a cue to it. For example, instead of *saying* "Sit, sit, sit!" as you try to get your dog to do so, why not wait until you are sure you can get him to sit by *luring* your dog to do so?

Hold a treat at your dog's nose and lift slightly up and back. Your dog's head will follow, and his rear will go to the ground.

Repeat this 5 to 10 times, at which point your dog should reliably and smoothly follow your hand movement and sit in response.

At this point, you are pretty sure you can get the "Sit," so say the word "sit" right before you move your hand. Doing so allows your dog to strongly associate the cue word with the actual behavior, not with an *attempt* for the behavior. By repeating the cue many times right before the behavior happens—and then by rewarding your dog for the appropriate behavior—you'll teach your dog which words are associated with the specific behavior in order to get rewarded.

a release word

By using a release word, you can tell your dog that he is finished with the behavior you asked him to do. A release word is sort of like a whistle at work that tells you it's time to go on break. However, the release word doesn't necessarily mean the training session is over—it only means that your dog can stop doing whatever you just asked him to do.

For example, if you ask your dog to lie down, how long should he stay there? You certainly don't want to stand over your dog repeating "Stay!" again and again, do you? So why not simply teach him that, when you ask him to lie down (or do anything else for that matter), you intend for him to lie down until you say the release word or until you ask him to do something else? You can choose any word to be your release word, but most trainers use "Okay" or "All Done."

chapter 2

training techniques: four roads to success

Because you have gotten control of the doggy resources, your dog is ready to pay attention to you. Now she can learn what you want her to learn–in order to earn the things that she wants. Your job is to teach her as efficiently and effectively as possible so that she has the best chance to earn her doggy resources and have fun playing the training game.

There are four ways to teach your dog to perform a behavior: capturing, shaping, luring and molding. The following is an explanation of each method and its pros and cons.

capture it!

Capturing a behavior means selectively rewarding any behavior that your dog offers on her own. For example, if your dog walks up and sits in front of you and you reward her for doing so, chances are she will try sitting again as a way to get another reward. Pretty soon, every time you take a step away from your dog and stand still, she will be likely to step toward you and sit. In this case, you have effectively *captured* a behavior your dog gave you all on her own.

Once the behavior (sitting) can be reliably predicted (in this instance, by your taking a step and then stopping), you can say a cue or command word right before the behavior is about to happen. In this case, right as you stop, say "Sit!" and your dog is likely to sit. At first, she will sit because she has learned that sitting in front of you is rewarding.

However, after you repeat the process of taking a step, saying "Sit!" and then stopping, your dog will make the connection that when you say "Sit!", it means she should put her rear on the ground to earn a reward. This connection will really sink in once you start to ignore sits she offers on her own and reward only those you request.

Capturing is a gentle, fun technique for training, especially for some tricks that might otherwise be difficult to get—such as wiping her face with her paw (or "Are You Bashful?"). The downside of capturing is that if you limit yourself to using just this technique, the early steps of dog training may take more time than necessary. For example, capturing a sit is easy, because most dogs will sit to look up at you if you are holding food. But capturing a "Down" may take quite a bit more time, since your dog is less likely to lie down and move her head away from the food in your hand if you stand in front of her and hold a treat. In this case it might be quicker to simply lure your dog to a "Down" (see "Lure It!", on page 27).

shape it!

Shaping is similar to capturing, but more step-oriented. With capturing, you wait for your dog to offer an entire behavior, such as sit, down, scratch or sneeze, before you reward her. With shaping, you reward your dog for giving you small steps in the right direction toward the entire desired behavior. Shaping is somewhat similar to playing the game of Hot and Cold in which you are given feedback about your behavior that tells you whether you are getting warmer or colder. This feedback is meant to *shape* you toward a desired result.

Shaping is very effective for rather complex behaviors. For example, if you want to teach your dog to circle, you can start by rewarding a slight head turn to the left or right. Then reward for a slightly more obvious turn, and so on until your dog makes a full circle. If you want to teach your dog to cover her eye with her front paw as though she were bashful, it is unlikely that she will offer the entire behavior in one fell swoop. Instead, you can shape the behavior by first rewarding even the slightest paw movement. After you reward the paw movement a number of times (the number of repetitions required will vary greatly depending on the individual dog and trainer), your dog will understand that moving her paw is what you want. Now you simply need to teach her that you want her to move her paw in a specific direction—in this case, toward her eye. Start being more selective about the paw movements that you reward, choosing only those that are gradually closer and closer to what you want.

Shaping is one of the best methods for trick training. It can move along very quickly, especially as you become a better trainer and your dog becomes a savvier student. The use of a marker (either a word or a clicker) is crucial when shaping behavior, because it gives you the ability to accurately mark the exact moment your dog takes the next small step in the right direction.

lure it!

A *lure* (usually a treat or toy) is an object that piques your dog's interest enough that she will follow it. By holding a lure in your hand at the tip of your dog's nose, you can move your dog's body into many positions. For example, hold a treat on the tip of your dog's nose and lift slightly up and back. Your dog will raise her head up and back to follow the lure, and in doing so, her rear will naturally go to the ground. Move the lure around your dog's body and you can get her to spin. Luring is a wonderful method for teaching the basics–"Sit," "Stand" and "Down"–because it is fast and easy enough for anybody to master, even children. Luring also can be useful in trick training, especially for tricks like "Sit Pretty" or "Sneaky Dog."

use it, then lose it!

If your goal is to teach your dog to respond reliably to a hand or verbal cue or command, it is important to fade out the lure so your dog learns to respond without it. If you don't fade the lure, you are likely to end up with a dog who only responds reliably when you have a treat or toy in your hand. Use the lure just long enough to help your dog to understand what you want her to do. But once your dog is reliably providing the correct behavior, you will want to fade out the lure so she learns to perform the behavior with only a hand cue (a subtler version of the lure) or a verbal cue. So once your dog reliably follows the lure and you have added the appropriate cue or command word (if luring for a "Sit," say "Sit!"; and if luring for a "Down," say "Down!") begin fading the lure.

You can effectively fade the lure if you:

- **Use the lure, but don't give it to your dog from the hand that lured her.** Instead, offer the reward from your other hand.
- **Make the lure movement without food in your hand and then offer the reward from your other hand.** If your dog doesn't respond to the hand signal, try again. If she still doesn't respond, try a time out. Ignore her for a moment or two, and then try again.
- **Make a slightly less obvious lure movement from your hand and then offer food from the other hand.** But keep in mind that each time you make the hand movement subtler, it changes the picture for your dog. Imagine if you were learning a new language and your teacher subtly changed the spelling of certain words. It might take you a moment or two to recognize them. The same holds true for your dog, although the "words" in this case are hand movements.

mold it!

Molding is using your hands–or a leash–to physically manipulate your dog into the desired position. For quite some time, the vast majority of dog-training books focused on using molding. While you certainly can use your hands to push and pull your dog into a "Sit," "Stand" or "Down," it is probably not the most pleasant method for your dog. Furthermore, it is not the most effective way to teach most tricks. For example, it would be difficult to mold your dog to wipe her eye with her paw, to march in place or to jump through your arms. However, very gentle molding can be helpful for getting your dog to perform tricks such as balancing a biscuit on her nose or offering her paw to shake.

combining techniques

You and your dog are most likely to achieve ultimate trick-training success if you become skilled at capturing, shaping, luring and very gentle molding. All are gentle, effective ways to teach, so keep an open mind and use one, two, three or all four ways to teach your dog a vast array of fun tricks.

chapter 3

building a solid foundation for tricks

Just as a well-built house has a solid foundation to offer good support, a well-trained trick dog should have a good grasp of the basics of obedience. The basic foundation for tricks are "Attention," "Sit," "Down" and "Stand." As with most of the tricks covered in this book, you have the option to use capturing, shaping, luring or very gentle molding when you teach these basic commands. However, I would suggest that most people lure for these basic commands, as it is the fastest way to get results.

attention

"Attention" is probably the most important basic obedience command. After all, it is unrealistic to teach any student (canine or human) that isn't paying attention to you. So the first step in trick training is to teach your dog to pay attention.

If you already have gotten control of the doggy resources (see "Playing the Training Game," in chapter 1), chances are you have seen a vast improvement in your dog's attention. After all, if your dog clearly understands that you are the source for all the things he wants in this world, how could he not pay attention to you?

However, while getting control of the doggy resources is a major step in the right direction toward getting your dog's attention, you should also teach your dog that when you say his name, it means you want him to look at you and wait for further instructions.

Ask your dog to sit in front of you or by your side. Hold a treat in your hand and move it from the tip of your dog's nose swiftly up to your eye. This way your dog will follow the food up to your eye. Mark and treat the moment he glances at you. Gradually increase the length of the glance from half a second to one second, and then to two seconds, three seconds and so on, by delaying the mark and treat for those lengths of time. When your dog holds your gaze reliably for five seconds or so, says his name right before you move the lure up to your eye. Then gradually fade the lure movement. For example, instead of bringing the lure in your hand all the way up to your eye, see if he will look up at you when you say his name and move your hand up to your chin. Then try to move your hand only to your chest. Eventually, you should be able to say his name and have him look at you without any lure at all.

sit

To lure a "Sit," hold the treat at your dog's nose. You can let him lick at the food treat in your hand, but don't let him have it yet. Move your hand slightly back toward your dog's rear and slightly up so your dog lifts his head back and slightly up to follow the food. As his head moves, his rear should go to the ground. It's like a seesaw–if one end goes up, the other goes down. Mark the behavior with "Yes" or a click and reward. Repeat many times during three- to five-minute training sessions. When your dog is easily and reliably sitting in response to your hand movement, say the cue word "Sit" right before you move your hand to lure.

Capturing a "Sit:" "Sit" is a very easy behavior to capture because most dogs are likely to sit when you walk up to them holding a treat because they will look up at you. When they look up, their rear is likely to go down.

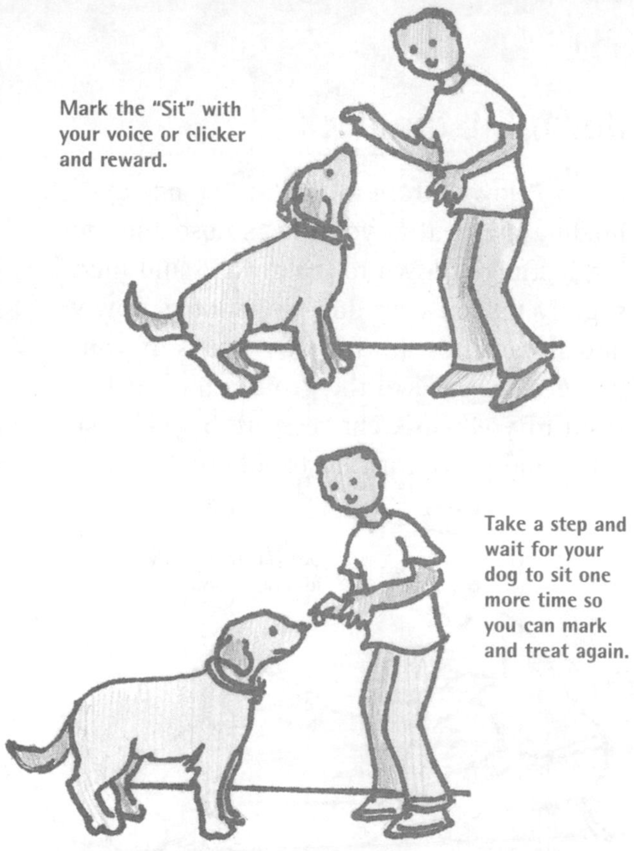

To capture a "Sit" without the lure, simply stand in front of your dog and wait for him to sit all on his own. Most dogs will do so quickly. Mark and treat the "Sit," then take a step away from your dog and wait for him to follow you and sit again. If he sits reliably when you take a step and stop, you should be able to predict when he will sit next. So say, "Sit!" as you stop, and then mark and reward the "Sit."

down/hit the deck

Lure a "Down" from a "Sit" or "Stand" by holding the treat at your dog's nose and moving it straight down to the ground and then slightly *toward* your dog so he looks down and slightly toward his front paws. If you move your hand to the ground too far in front of your dog, chances are he will just stand and move forward to follow it.

Get your dog ready to lure a "Down."

Make sure to hold the lure just below your dog's nose so that he must lie down to get it.

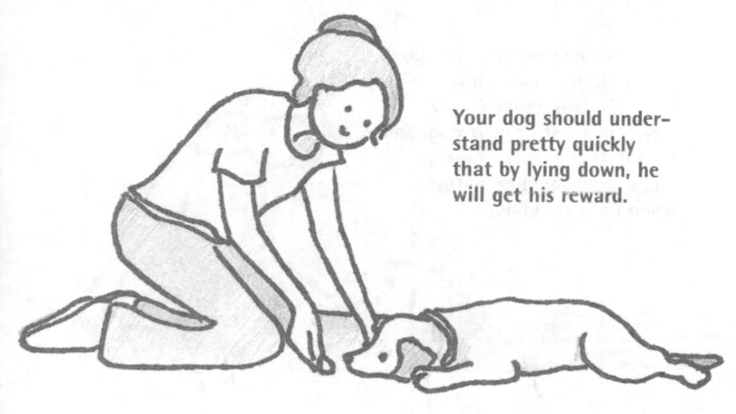

Your dog should understand pretty quickly that by lying down, he will get his reward.

Mark and treat when he lies down. When your dog reliably follows the lure to the ground and lies down, say the cue word "Down!" right before you lure. You can also try to capture the "Down" by waiting until your dog offers it on his own and then marking and treating him for doing so. However, in most cases it is much easier to lure a "Down" than to wait to capture.

stand

You should teach your dog to "Stand" on cue because it's the basis of tricks such as "Take a Bow" and "Sit Pretty." Standing can also be helpful at veterinary examinations and grooming sessions. This is the way most show dog handlers teach dogs to stand in the ring when they are being examined by the judge.

Lure your dog to "Sit" and hold a treat to his nose. Move your hand forward about 6 to 12 inches in front of your dog, and hold it at the level where your dog's nose would be naturally when he is standing.

Your dog should follow the lure into the "Stand," at which point you should mark and treat.

When he reliably follows the lure,
say the cue word "Stand!" right
before you lure him to "Stand."

chapter 4

let the games begin!

choosing the right tricks for your dog

The easiest way to be successful training tricks from day one is to choose tricks that are appropriate for your dog. Some dogs are very athletic and can do just about anything from twirling on command to leaping through your arms. Other dogs may be limited by their body type, age or health, and are best focused on tricks that require less exertion such as "Shake!", "Bang!" and "Take a Bow!"

Just as you would consult your doctor before beginning a new exercise regimen, it is advisable to consult your dog's veterinarian before your pet starts her new training regimen. You will want to discuss how much physical exercise and what types of activities are best suited to your dog.

touch/target

"Targeting" is one of the most basic and useful behaviors you can teach your dog. Teaching your dog to touch your hand or the tip of a target stick on request will make teaching more complex behaviors easier. If your dog knows to "Target" on cue, you can substitute that for a lure to teach many of the tricks described in this book. But, "Targeting" is also useful for basic manners. For example, if you want to ask your dog to move to a certain spot, you can do so by moving your hand there and asking her to "Target" to it.

Goal: To teach your dog to touch her nose to your hand or the tip of a target stick on cue

Foundation: Attention

Technique: Capturing, shaping or luring

Hold the target (your hand or stick) near your dog at nose level. Don't push it into your dog's face—your goal is to teach your dog to touch it, not to have her learn to accept being touched by it. Have the target close enough that your dog doesn't have to walk far to get to it. Most dogs will touch your hand or the tip of the stick when it is presented to them, if only out of curiosity. Mark and treat when she does so.

Hold the target near your dog at nose level.

Mark and treat for any movement closer to the target.
touch!
Say the cue words "Touch" or "Target" right before you present your hand or the target stick.

If your dog doesn't touch the target immediately, you'll need to shape her behavior. To begin, mark and treat for even a glance at the target, be it your hand or the target stick. After a few repetitions, raise the reward criteria and mark and treat for movement closer to the target until your dog eventually touches it. She will then learn that touching the target is what earns a mark and a treat!

You can also lure for this behavior by holding a treat in your hand to encourage your dog to sniff it. Or have a treat in your other hand (not the one the dog is supposed to target to), and hold it behind your open palm of the target hand. Once your dog is touching your hand reliably, stop using the other hand behind it with food as a lure. Then try moving your hand a few inches away so she needs to make more of an effort to reach it. Gradually make it harder for your dog to reach your hand (moving farther away and to the left or right).

When your dog is reliably making an effort to touch the target when it is presented to her, say the cue word "Touch" or "Target" right before you present your hand or the target stick. This way, the request to "Target" on command will be strongly associated with the behavior of "Targeting."

lights out!

Goal: To teach your dog to turn off a light switch on command

Foundation: Targeting

Technique: Targeting and shaping

"Lights Out" is appropriate for smaller dogs who can reach a light switch by hopping onto a chair in front of it and then stand up to touch it, or for larger dogs who can stand on their hind legs to reach the switch.

Touch the light switch with your target stick and then ask your dog to touch the stick.

Give your dog a chance to play around so she can figure out which way is easiest for her to turn off the light.

If your dog is small- or medium-size and needs to be on a chair to reach the light switch, it is best to work on teaching your dog to hop onto the chair before attempting to teach her to flip the switch. First, teach her to hop onto the chair by luring her or verbally encouraging her to do so. Then mark and reward the behavior. Once your dog is comfortable hopping onto the chair, you can begin working on teaching her to flip the switch.

Simply touch the target stick to the switch and ask your dog to "Touch" or "Target," depending on which cue you have taught. Some dogs find it easier to use their paw to turn off the light switch, while others prefer to use their nose. At first, she may only touch the switch rather than actually flip it. Begin by marking and rewarding for any contact with the switch. Once she is enthusiastically touching the switch, start to be more selective about the touches you reward. Mark and reward those that are most likely to move the switch (see "Shape It!", on page 26).

When your dog is reliably turning on the light switch, stop using the target stick. Stand near the switch and encourage your dog to stand near it as well. Your dog may seem confused for a moment, because the target stick is no longer present as an aid. But, chances are after a moment or two, she will figure out what you want her to do. Mark and reward her for touching or flipping the light switch. When she is doing so reliably, say the cue word right before you see her move to touch the switch.

basic retrieve

Goal: To teach your dog to retrieve objects on command

Foundation: Attention

Technique: Shaping

Some dogs have a strong natural inclination to retrieve objects. However, even dogs bred for specific retrieving abilities should first learn to retrieve reliably while on leash. Keeping your dog on a leash means she won't get the opportunity to learn to run off with objects that she should be bringing back to you. As cute as it may look to see a young puppy grabbing a toy and running off with it—as if to say, "It's mine!"—this behavior ruins the retrieve game. It might even be the seed of potential possessive aggression issues.

Start teaching this trick with your dog on a six-foot leash, and use one of your dog's favorite toys as her first retrieve object. Show your dog the toy and toss it about five feet away. As soon as she grabs the toy in her mouth, use verbal praise and encourage her to bring it back to you. When she gets to you, mark and treat or simply toss it again. For some dogs, the toss of the toy is reward enough, and there is no need to offer a food treat. As with most tricks, it is usually best to limit practice sessions to about three to five minutes. This way your dog is likely to remain enthusiastic for the game.

Use one of your dog's favorite toys as her first retrieve object.

Show your dog her toy and then toss it about five feet away.

If your dog retrieves reliably and enthusiastically at a distance of about 20 feet, you can try playing the retrieve game without the leash.

Gradually increase the distance you toss your dog's toy. At this point you can let the leash drag behind your dog or remove it entirely. But if your dog starts to run off with the object, be sure to put the leash back on and help her understand the rules of the game.

shake!

Goal: To teach your dog to raise her paw in the air to "Shake," "Wave" or offer a "High Five"

Foundation: Sit

Technique: Luring, capturing, shaping or molding

Some dogs naturally use their paws to solicit attention and other resources, especially if you sit on the floor with with some treats.

Mark and treat when your dog raises her paw and allows you to gently hold it.

If you handle your dog's paws when she is a pup, it will be much easier to touch them when she is all grown up.

Capture the paw movement by marking and treating the moment your dog's paw goes into the air. After a few three- to five-minute training sessions, mark and treat when your dog raises her paw and allows you to gently hold it. You can also lure a paw shake by holding a bit of food in your hand at your dog's nose. Move it to the left or right side of your dog so she leans to one side or the other to follow it. This movement will cause her to be slightly off balance and lift her paw off the ground. Mark and treat when she does so.

Be aware that some dogs' paws are sensitive enough that simply touching or tickling their paw will cause them to lift it. This can work to your favor if you gently touch your dog's paw and then she raises it. But if she is this sensitive to your touch, it is likely she won't like to have her paw gently held as a shake gesture. In this case, simply spend a few training sessions offering a treat each time your dog allows you to gently touch her paw. Before you know it, she'll love it!

Note: It is a good idea to work on teaching your dog to be comfortable having all body parts handled before you begin trick training.

high five

Goal: To teach your dog to raise her paw to make contact with your palm

Foundation: Shake

Technique: Luring, capturing or shaping

Once you have taught your dog to "Shake," move your hand about an inch higher than you have been holding it for the shake trick. This way, your dog has to make more of an effort to make contact with your hand. Gradually raise your hand until it is high enough to look like your dog is giving you a high five. Be sure not to ask your dog to raise it so high that it becomes uncomfortable for her shoulder joints and muscles. At the same time, gradually turn your hand so it is facing your dog as opposed to having your palm up as you do when asking your dog to shake.

are you bashful?

Goal: To teach your dog to cover her eye or nose with one paw

Foundation: Sit

Technique: Capturing or shaping

For some dogs, the quickest way to teach this trick is to simply blow in their face. This may cause them to wipe their face–or muzzle–with their paw. If this works, mark and treat for the face wipe and then gradually decrease the strength of your blow until your dog moves her paw for just a very subtle movement of your mouth toward her face. At this point, you can say the cue as you lean in slightly to your dog.

The quickest way to teach this trick is to gently blow in your dog's face.

Reward the slightest paw movements toward your dog's face.

And don't forget to reward your dog.

If this doesn't work (blowing in their faces makes some dogs sneeze!) but you have already tackled "Shake," your dog is likely to offer you a paw movement anyway because she has already learned that doing so might earn her a reward. In this case, simply shape what she offers you into a face swipe. Start by marking and treating any paw movement you get and then start to be more selective about what you reward. Reward the paw movements that come closest to your dog's face. This means you have to watch carefully and be discriminating. However, don't be so careful that you forget to reward your dog occasionally.

If you are too picky in what you are looking for—and if you fail to reward for something in the correct direction of a full face wipe—your dog might get frustrated and shut down. Don't forget, learning something new can be confusing and a little stressful. Support your dog and be a generous rewarder!

achoo!/please sneeze

Goal: To teach your dog to sneeze on cue

Foundation: Attention

Technique: Capturing

This trick is taught in a similar manner to teaching your dog "Are You Bashful?". Some dogs will make a light sneeze if you gently blow in their face. Mark and treat the sneeze and try again. As the training sessions progress, work on decreasing the blow until all you have to do is make a slight blowing gesture. When you can reliably predict that your dog is about to sneeze, say the cue word right before you prompt her to sneeze. And then get ready to say, "Gesundheit!"

If your dog doesn't sneeze in response to a gentle blow in her face, you might need to simply wait until she sneezes on her own to capture it. When she sneezes, mark the behavior and reward. A dog who is trick savvy–that is, she has learned that offering behaviors is rewarding–is likely to try to get another reward from you. If you're lucky, one of the behaviors she tries may be a little sneeze. If so, mark and treat. If not, simply wait for the next time she sneezes and try again.

it's a stickup/sit pretty

Goal: To teach your dog to balance on her hind end and raise her front paws in the air

Foundation: Sit

Technique: Capturing, shaping, luring or very gentle molding

Start this trick with your dog sitting in a corner. This way, your dog will have two walls supporting her frame.

Sit directly in front of your dog or slightly off to one side. Hold a bit of food to the tip of her nose as you slowly lift it up and back.

Once your dog can balance with only the corner supporting her, see if you can move her just an inch or two away from the wall.

This trick requires your dog to have good balance and strong back and leg muscles. It is usually easiest for dogs whose backs are not very long in relation to their height (although I have worked with a few Dachshunds who do a wonderful "Sit Pretty").

Many small dogs will offer this behavior consistently on their own. In this case, it is easy to capture, mark and reward. However, if your dog is not offering this behavior on her own, luring is probably your best option. Sit directly in front of your dog or slightly off to one side. Hold a bit of food on the tip of her nose as you slowly lift it up and back. Be careful not to raise your hand too high too fast or your dog will simply jump up for the food. She should just begin to lift her front end off the ground to reach your hand. Mark and treat for even a little movement upward. Going slowly and rewarding for even very small steps in the right direction gives your dog the chance to build her balance and offers you a better chance for success.

You might discover that your dog needs help balancing her front end as well, so get ready to let her rest her front feet on your outstretched arm to start with. Move your hand away a bit once your dog lifts her front end off the ground with confidence. Be prepared for this to take many repetitions before your dog can get her balance. Again, be a generous rewarder!

Once your dog is confidently and reliably following the lure or sitting on her haunches with her front legs off the ground on her own, you can say the cue word right before the behavior is about to happen (either by your luring or her doing it on her own). Then mark and treat for success.

say your prayers

Goal: To teach your dog to rest her front paws on an object and lower her head between her paws

Foundation: Sit

Technique: Capturing, luring or shaping

It is best to separate this trick into two parts, first teaching your dog to rest her paws on an object, and then teaching her to lower her head between her feet. The object can be a table, chair or small box for small dogs.

You can shape this behavior by rewarding your dog for any contact with the chair or box. Then reward her for making contact with the chair or box with her paws. You can also lure the behavior by putting a treat on the chair or box to entice your dog to put her paws up on the seat. Placing the treat near the back of the chair or box is usually the best way to get your dog to place her paws all the way up.

When she is reliably resting her paws on the edge of the chair (or whichever object you have chosen to use for this trick), work on building up the length of time your dog holds the behavior before marking and treating.

Start with just two seconds and then increase to three, four, five and so forth. When she can hold the behavior for approximately 10 seconds, you can teach her to lower her head between her feet.

Shape the behavior by rewarding your dog for even slight downward movements of her head until her head is eventually all the way between her front paws. You can also lure the behavior by holding a bit of food below your dog and between her feet so she looks down to get the food. Mark and treat when she does this.

Once she is comfortable resting her head between her front paws, gradually increase the length of time you ask your dog to hold the position before marking and treating. The release word for this trick can be "Amen!"

sneaky dog

Goal: To teach your dog to crawl on the ground, with her chest remaining low

Foundation: Down and Targeting

Technique: Luring

Position yourself on the floor slightly ahead of your dog and ask her to lie down. Make sure your dog is lying in a prone down, squarely on both hind hips.

Place your hand on the ground at your dog's nose. Move your hand slightly forward. If your dog scoots along the ground even a few inches to follow your hand, mark and treat. Try again and encourage her to move forward a bit farther. If it is easier for you, use the target stick so that you don't have to reach ahead of your dog. Sit by your dog's side, place the tip of the target stick an inch or two in front of her and follow the instructions as if you were using your hand as a lure. If your dog gets up, simply ask or lure her to lie down and try again.

Use the lure to move your dog's head a little to one side or the other.

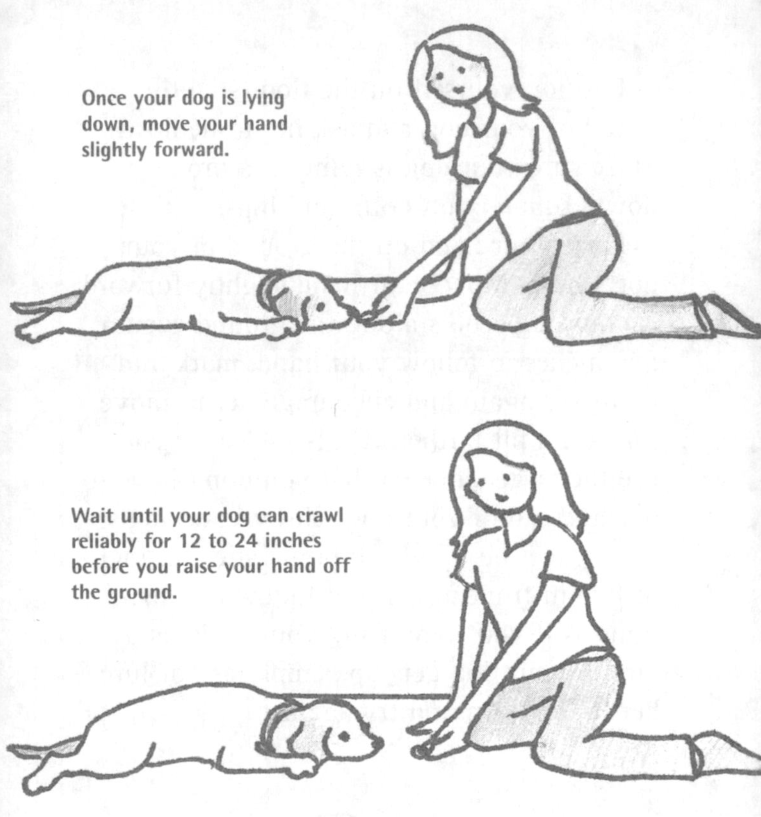
Once your dog is lying down, move your hand slightly forward.

Wait until your dog can crawl reliably for 12 to 24 inches before you raise your hand off the ground.

As an aid to help your dog understand to stay low to the ground rather than to stand up to follow your hand, you can place your other hand gently on your dog's withers (just between her shoulder blades). Do not press down on your dog to keep her on the ground. Your hand is only meant to be a gentle aid. You can also have your dog crawl below your bent knees as you sit on the ground. If your dog is large, have her crawl beneath a coffee table. When your dog crawls reliably for 12 to 24 inches, gradually raisc your hand off the ground and give her the "Crawl" hand signal while you stand.

bang!/play dead

Goal: To teach your dog to lie still and flat on her side (or with her legs in the air) until you release her

Foundation: Down

Technique: Luring or shaping

Start from the "Down" with a bit of food in your hand.

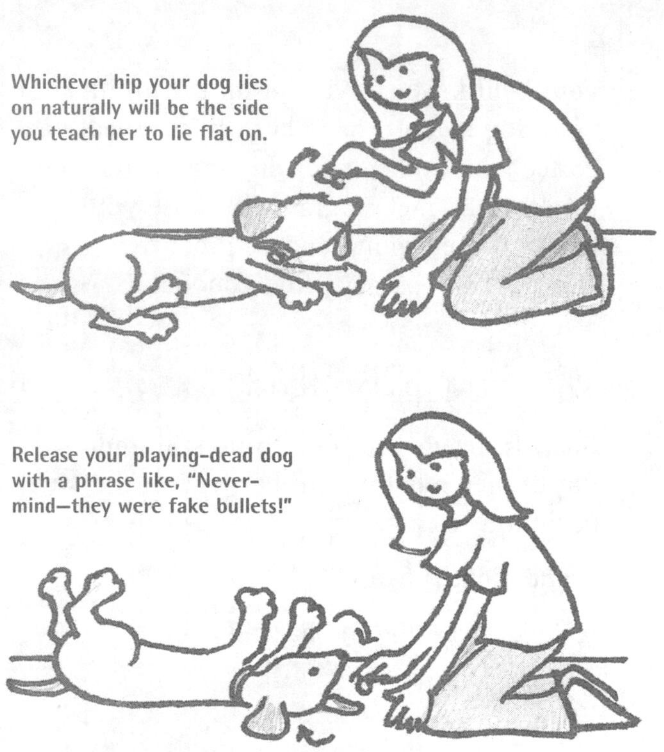

Whichever hip your dog lies on naturally will be the side you teach her to lie flat on.

Release your playing-dead dog with a phrase like, "Never-mind—they were fake bullets!"

From the "Down," use a bit of food in your hand and lure your dog to lie flat on her side by gently moving the food toward your dog's head—this will cause her to lay her head on the ground. Keep your hand as low to the ground as possible and mark and treat. The next time, lure her so she is lying flat on her side, but wait one second before marking and treating and releasing her to jump up from the "Down." Work up to about 7 to 10 seconds before the mark and treat.

roll over/leftovers

Goal: To teach your dog to roll over one way and then back the other.

Foundation: Down

Technique: Luring, capturing or shaping

Ask your dog to lie down. If she is lying in a prone "Down" (even on both hips, as opposed to resting more on one hip or the other), lure her to rest on one hip or the other by turning your hand slowly to one side or the other. From there, gently push your hand toward your dog's nose so that her head goes back and she lies flat on her side. Now move your hand slowly over her head to the other side of her body. As she begins to follow your hand and turn her body over, you might try gently tickling her inner thigh. This may get her to open her hind legs and swing them over as well.

First, ask your dog to lie down.

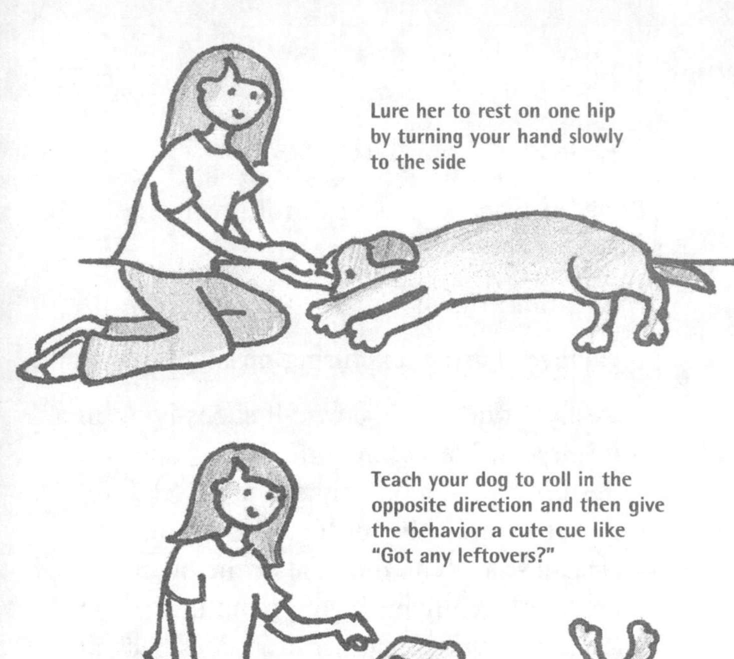

Some dogs are not comfortable lying in a vulnerable position on their backs. If your dog seems hesitant to roll, try shaping the behavior by rewarding for small movements toward the intended goal. If your dog enjoys rolling on the grass or on a thick carpet in an effort to get a nice back scratch, you can also try capturing the behavior when she is introduced to one of these surfaces. Once you can reliably predict that the roll will happen, say the cue word right before it does.

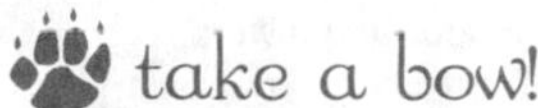

take a bow!

Goal: To teach your dog to lower her front end (keeping her rear raised) so she looks like she is bowing

Foundation: Stand

Technique: Capturing, shaping or luring

Most dogs will stretch when they wake up or occasionally play bow to solicit play. In either case, take the opportunity to capture the behavior and let your dog know that it is added to the list of things that are potentially rewarding for her.

A doggy bow is usually an easy behavior to capture.

To avoid confusion between the verbal signals "Bow!" and "Down!" (which may sound similar to your dog), try a verbal cue like "Take a Bow!" or "Curtsy!"

When the light bulb goes off in your dog's head and she figures out that bowing is what you want, she will start to do so more consistently during the training session. Mark and reward for each bow, and pretty soon she will bow immediately after you offer her a treat because she knows at that moment it is the way to get more treats. You can also lure this behavior by asking your dog to stand and then lowering your hand to the ground.

Your dog's front end should follow your hand to the ground. But be prepared to mark and treat the exact moment it does so, because she may go all the way to the ground to a "Down" position. It may take her a few sessions to understand it is a "Bow" you want and not a "Down." Be patient and watch carefully for the "Bow" so you can mark it the moment it happens.

You may also avoid confusion between the "Bow" and the "Down" by spending time working on the "Down" from a "Sit" only, whereas the "Bow" will always be from a "Stand." And, last but not least, sit on the ground or in a low chair when you first teach the "Bow." This way, your dog is not likely to raise her head very high to look at you (as she might if you were standing). If you are standing, she may raise her head to look up—and this may make her rear go to the ground.

Once you can reliably get the "Bow"—either because your dog is freely offering the behavior or because you are luring it—begin saying the cue word right before the bow happens.

Once your dog bows reliably in response to your cue, work on ignoring bows offered wihout the cue and increasing the duration of the "Bow" by pausing for a second before the mark and treat. Repeat the one-second "Bow" for about five repetitions, and then try for a two-second "Bow" by pausing for two seconds before the mark and treat. Gradually increase the pause to five seconds or so, and end the trick with a cute release phrase like "OK, get off the stage!"

beep-beep-beep-beep!

Goal: To teach your dog to step backward on command

Foundation: Stand

Technique: Luring and shaping

You can teach this trick by standing in front of your dog and taking one step toward her. If she backs up, mark and treat. If she looks up at you and sits, try holding a treat at your dog's nose and lowering it slightly downwards toward her chest as you step toward her. Or hold the target stick at her chest as you step toward her and ask her to touch it. This way, she is less likely to sit because she won't be looking up at you.

Once she is moving back one step easily, try for two and then three. Once your dog is moving back five to six steps smoothly, add the chosen cue word right before you prompt the behavior with a step toward her. Repeat this throughout many short training sessions and gradually try to fade the aid of your body moving toward her as a cue until she will eventually back up on the verbal cue alone.

Note: If your dog is having a hard time backing up in a straight line, try practicing with her standing parallel to a wall. This way she is more likely to move straight back.

 speak!

Goal: For your dog to learn to bark or howl on command

Foundation: Attention

Technique: Capturing, luring or shaping

One of the easiest ways to get a dog to "Speak" is to have someone ring the front doorbell. Have your dog on a leash by your side, and have a friend on the other side of the front door. Say whichever cue word you have chosen (for example, "Speak!"), and tell your friend in advance to ring the bell right as she hears you say the cue word. Reward your dog for barking, and then ask for quiet by waving a tasty treat in front of her nose.

She will stop barking as she sniffs and nibbles the treat. Repeat this many times until your cue word becomes as powerful a cue to bark as the cue of the doorbell itself.

One of the added benefits of teaching your dog this trick is that it gives you the ability to control your dog's barking. By teaching her to bark, you can also teach her to stop barking. As you wave the treat by her nose after she barks, ask her to "Shush!" The food should distract her from what made her bark. Mark and treat for even a second of quiet. Gradually increase the time from when you ask her to "Shush!" to when you mark and treat so that she learns to be quiet for longer and longer periods of time.

Tether your dog by leash to a stable object such as a doorknob, heavy table or chest. Use the front doorbell as an aid to entice your dog to bark.

Reward your dog for barking, and then ask her for quiet by waving a tasty treat in front of her nose.

circle left & circle right, spin, spin, spin

Goal: To teach your dog to circle to the left and right

Foundation: Stand

Technique: Luring, shaping or capturing

Some dogs will naturally circle when they are excited—for example, when you pick up the leash to take them for a walk. If your dog reacts this way, capture the behavior by marking and treating for the spin.

You can lure and shape a spin in either direction by holding a food lure at your dog's noseand moving it to the left or right toward your dog's rear so she turns her head to follow the food. Some dogs will follow a lure all the way around in a full circle. If so, mark and reward. If your dog is hesitant to turn her whole body, shape the behavior by marking and rewarding her for turning her head to follow your hand, then for turning her head and shoulder and so on until she makes a full turn.

Once she is turning smoothly and without hesitation, say the cue word right before you move your hand to lure her or right before she spins on her own. At this point, be sure to reward her only if you ask her to spin, not if she does it on her own. This way, she learns it is spinning on your cue, not when she wants to, that is rewarding.

As with all tricks, gradually fade the visual prompt of moving your hand around her body. That is, make the circling gesture around her body more and more subtle. With practice you should be able to ask her to spin with just a verbal cue or a subtle physical cue of your hand making a little spin motion.

You can take this trick a step further by asking your dog to circle around a pole and using a cue like "What do you do on May Day?" You can also teach your dog to turn in the other direction, but be sure to use a different cue for each direction.

leave it!

Goal: To teach your dog to allow you to place a treat on her paw and not touch it

Foundation: Down or Sit

Technique: Shaping

Start with your dog in a "Down" at your side. Hold a dry treat in each hand. At the same time bring both hands to the ground–one right to your dog's mouth and the other to the ground about one foot in front of your dog.

Let your dog take a quick little lick or nibble of the treat that's near her mouth. Repeat this about 20 times. Each movement of your hands to the ground should take about half a second, so this series of 20 repetitions should take about 10 seconds.

Now bring the hand that is placing the treat on the ground away from your dog down about half a second sooner than the hand that is going to your dog's mouth. If your dog pops up to go for the food that is farther away from her, just quickly pick it up and get her to lie down again.

Let your dog take a quick little lick or nibble of the treat that's near her mouth.

Now bring the hand that is placing the treat on the floor farther away from your dog.

Have your dog ignore the food on her paw for up to 30 seconds.

Your dog will eventually learn the only thing that happens if she tries to go for the "farther-away-food," is that it goes away. Gradually increase the pause between when the "farther-away-food," goes down before the food nearest to her from half a second sooner, to one second sooner, to two seconds sooner, and so on.

Be sure to take a lot of breaks. Don't expect your dog to lie down for more than a total of one minute or so. When your dog is able to leave the food alone for 15 seconds at a foot away, work on bringing it closer to her. Just be sure that as you bring the food closer to your dog–which makes it harder for her to resist eating it–you decrease the amount of time you expect her to ignore it.

Move the food about one inch closer and try to have her ignore it for three seconds. Then gradually build back up to 15 seconds. Decrease the distance by another inch and begin again with three seconds of her ignoring it before you build the time back up. Repeat this process in three- to five-minute training sessions until the food is on her paw and she can hold it there for 30 seconds or so.

balance a biscuit

Goal: To teach your dog to balance a biscuit on her nose until you release her, at which point she tosses it in the air and catches it

Foundation: Sit and Leave It

Technique: Shaping

It is a good idea to break this trick into two parts. The first part has your dog balancing the biscuit on her nose. The second part has her tossing the biscuit in the air and then catching it. For the first part, make sure to teach your dog "Leave It" with a biscuit on the ground in front of her (as in the previous trick) before you teach her to "Leave It" with a biscuit on her nose. For the second part, make sure she can catch treats when you toss them to her.

Now ask your dog to sit in front of you. Gently hold her muzzle as you place a small biscuit on her nose. It is usually best to place the biscuit lengthwise on the flattest part of her muzzle (close to the end so it is easier for her to balance it, and eventually to toss and catch it).

Once the biscuit is in place, try to remove your hand just a little away from her muzzle.

But still keep your hand relatively close so she is less likely to move. Don't expect your dog to balance the biscuit for more than a second or two. Mark the behavior, then take the biscuit off her nose and reward her.

Gradually increase the length of time you ask your dog to balance the biscuit. But continue to keep your hand close to her muzzle as an aid. When she is able to hold the biscuit for five to seven seconds, try moving your hand a little farther away.

Once your dog balances the biscuit reliably for five to seven seconds with your hand completely away from her muzzle, you can start teaching her to toss and catch the biscuit in the air. If you say her release word in an excited tone, chances are that she will pop her head up, the biscuit will fly into the air and she probably will catch it. If she is having a hard time catching the biscuit midair, just practice this part of the trick separately for a while. You might also try experimenting with different sizes and types of food that are easier for your dog to balance and catch. Your dog is sure to enjoy this part of the game!

appendix

training resources

Once you become involved in trick training your dog, you may want to have more information at your fingertips. Following are basic resources–books, websites and e-mail lists–that you can refer to so both human and canine are well prepared to carry on the training game.

books

Arden, Andrea. *Dog-Friendly Dog Training.* New York: Howell Book House, 1999.

Dunbar, Ian, PhD, MRCVS. *How to Teach a New Dog Old Tricks.* Berkeley, California: James and Kenneth Publishers, 1998.

Pryor, Karen. *Don't Shoot the Dog: The New Art of Teaching and Training.* New York: Bantam Books, 1999.

——. *Getting Started: Clicker Training for Dogs.* Waltham, Massachusetts: Sunshine Books, 2001.

websites

www.AndreaArden.com
www.DogTraining101.com
www.DogIQ.com
www.NoMoreBarking.com
www.Housetraining.com
www.Petmate.com

finding a trainer

Visit the website for The Association of Pet Dog Trainers at www.APDT.com.

email lists

Trickdog: trickdog-subscribe@yahoogroups.org
ClickerSolutions: clickersolutions-subscribe@yahoo.org